GODALM

A Short Hist

Godalming in 1871.

GODALMING
A Short History

John Janaway

AMMONITE BOOKS
GODALMING

Acknowledgements

Many thanks to Ron Head, Mary Pritchard, Matthew Alexander, Nicholas Battle, my friends and colleagues at the Surrey Local Studies Library and last, but never least, to my wife Sue.

First published 1983 as *The Story of Godalming* by Local Heritage Books
This edition published by Ammonite Books 1993

ISBN 1 869866 08 8

Printed and bound in the United Kingdom by Staples Printers Rochester Limited Neptune Close, Medway City Estate, Frindsbury, Rochester, Kent ME2 4LT

Contents

To Percy Woods (1842-1922)
a pioneer local historian

Preface

Godalming must seem to many to be a town which only the clamour of the twentieth century has awoken from perennial slumber. A place with an uneventful history and little claim to fame beyond its narrow streets. Nothing could be further from the truth. The story of this small town, set in the beautiful countryside of West Surrey, is full of fascination and surprise. A town of industry, a town with many famous sons and at least one international 'first' to its name.

This book makes no claim to be an exhaustive history of Godalming. For that considerably more research and space would be needed. However, for the first time in one volume, the main threads of the history of this unique town and its thriving community are drawn together.

John Janaway
October 1993

Origins

The town of Godalming is situated on the northern edge of some of the most beautiful countryside in England. To the south a succession of Greensand hills rise up to reach their maximum height at Hindhead. These hills are dissected by the headwaters of the River Wey. The north branch of the river rises on the chalk near Alton in Hampshire and flows northeast through the ancient castle town of Farnham before turning east to join the south branch, whose source is near Haslemere, at Tilford. Near Tilford are the ruins of Waverley Abbey and in its heyday the Abbey was undoubtedly one of the major influences on the area. Between Farnham and Guildford, the river is crossed by a series of bridges which probably date from the thirteenth century and may have been built by the monks from the abbey. At Eashing there is a particularly well preserved example of one of these bridges and here the river turns northeast, where it has cut a gorge through the flat-topped hills of the erosion resistant Bargate Beds.

At the exit of this beautiful and unspoilt part of the river valley the Wey is joined by a small tributary, the River Ock. Immediately downstream of this confluence, the valley begins to broaden out a little, and it is here that the town of Godalming was established. The attractive narrow streets of the town lie on a well-drained platform just above the flood plain of the river. The steep-sided tree-clad hills form a backcloth which adds greatly to the rural setting of the town. It was not always so, and many people who know the area well would be surprised to learn that the majority of these trees have grown up during the last hundred years.

The main High Street of Godalming is built on the sandy Hythe Beds of the Lower Greensand. The name 'Hythe' is derived from the town of that name on the coast of Kent where the same deposits are particularly well exposed. These beds, mainly consisting of sands with some chert, date to the Cretaceous Period and are about a hundred million years old. The hills surrounding the town are capped with Bargate Beds. The origin of this name is obscure but it has been suggested that it comes from Burgate, a locality to the south near Hascombe. The Bargate Beds are a local development of the Sandgate Beds (again from Kent) and the exposures within a three mile radius of the town are unique. The deposit consists of sand, pebbles and hard calcareous sandstone which is found in irregular masses in the beds, each lump of stone being given the old quarryman's name of a 'dogger'. Quarrying of the Bargate Stone was an important industry until well into the present century.

At the Bridge Street end of the town are to be found alluvial deposits of fine sand and silt laid down not only by the River Wey as it meandered its course across the meadows but also by small streams coming down from the hills. One of these formerly flowed down part of Bridge Street and was responsible for giving that street its earlier name of The Stream or Watery Lane. At the other end of the town in the Mint Street and Mill Lane area there are alluvial deposits of sand and flint gravel. These deposits lie between the Rivers Ock and Wey and it is on this well-drained triangle of land, near the junction of the two rivers, that the Saxons probably established the first Godalming settlement. However, although there is as yet no archaeological evidence for this first settlement, despite two small excavations undertaken recently, much has been discovered in the area surrounding the town to prove that man has been active here for several thousand years. The landscape we see today has developed during more than five thousand years of human activity.

The Palaeolithic Period of the Stone Age represents the earliest period of man's development when he first learnt to make tools to perform specific functions, an activity which immediately separates him from other members of the animal kingdom. A hard siliceous rock derived from the chalk proved to be one of the most suitable materials for the manufacture of the various tools a hunting man required. In flint, man

Mill Lane leading to Hatch Mill, about 1895.

discovered something which was to be of basic importance to him for thousands of years. A flint tool is almost indestructable and, once discarded by its maker, will survive in the soil to become, in many cases, the only remaining evidence of early man. In recent times thousands of palaeolithic hand axes have been re-discovered and no museum is without its collection of these tools. Hundreds were found in gravel pits near Farnham, mainly in the last century, but few have been discovered in the Godalming area. However, one is recorded from Peasemarsh to the north.

After the end of the last Ice Age, the climate gradually improved and the treeless open tundra gave way to forests of birch and pine and finally of oak, elm and alder. The characteristic tools of the Mesolithic peoples who inhabited these forests were the microlith, tiny worked flints which were used in a number of ways such as barbs for wooden harpoons, and the tranchet axe which was a very effective tool for cutting wood. Examples of these tools have been found in various places near the town.

Some time before 3000 BC man's whole pattern of life began to change with the introduction of farming and stock-keeping. Gradually the somewhat nomadic life gave way to a more settled existence and in its wake there followed a succession of technological developments. These developments included the making of pottery, though the use of flint for weapons and tools continued. Neolithic flints have been found in some numbers on the local hills and especially at sites near Westbrook and Upper Eashing to the west and southwest of Godalming. They have also been recently found in excavations at Angel Court in the heart of the town. Little evidence has been discovered so far in the area for Bronze Age man who lived in the period following the Neolithic and made first use of metals. Two early bronze flat axes were found in Farncombe to the north and in Charterhouse Museum there are some later socketed axes which were discovered locally many years ago.

It is reasonable to presume that the light but fairly rich soils of the area came under extensive cultivation during the Iron Age (c.500 BC). Material from this period has been found at Charterhouse and Binscombe and to the south is the hillfort at Hascombe. The construction of a hillfort such as Hascombe implies a high degree of social organisation amongst the peoples of the area during the Iron Age. The Iron Age population were skilled farmers and traders as well as warriors. Trade by barter had, to some extent at least, given way to an organised system of gold coinage. Two such gold coins, copying the Philip of Macedon stater, were found near the River Wey at Godalming during the middle of the last century. After the Roman invasion of 43 AD the indigenous Celtic population gradually became Romanised and adopted most of the culture of that civilisation whilst still retaining many Celtic characteristics. No evidence for a Romano-British occupation of the actual site of present Godalming has been found barring one small sherd of pottery recently discovered at Angel Court. However, the area was ringed by villas or farmsteads and undoubtedly intensively cultivated during this period. Evidence of Romano-British occupation has been found at Charterhouse, Compton, Puttenham, Chiddingfold and Binscombe (excavated during the 1950s and 60s). At Hurtmore, very recent finds, mainly of pottery, point to an occupation site yet to be discovered.

The period immediately following the crumbling of the Roman civilisation in Britain in the fifth century as yet lacks any solid evidence upon which to base the story of the Godalming area at that time. We know that the Saxons may have occupied this part of the Wey Valley in the late sixth or seventh century. Unfortunately, of the 150 years or so which preceeded this occupation, nothing is known. It is likely that the breakdown of the Romano-British civilisation was a gradual degeneration over many decades. Many of the population may well have clung to the shreds of the old civilisation until the end of the 5th century. Whatever the real truth of the history of this period, we do know for certain that the Saxon culture gained the ascendancy and that the name which our town still bears is of Saxon origin.

What was the origin of that name and when was the first settlement

This 1779 view shows the medieval town bridge, replaced by the present one in 1782.

made? A number of theories have been put forward over the years to explain the derivation of the name 'Godalming'. The most likely and now generally accepted one is that it means 'Godhelm's Ingas' which roughly translates as 'the land of the people or clan of Godhelm'. Other theories include Godhelm's field or meadow and 'Godiva's stream' – after a prioress of that name who held a priory in the town. This would certainly not be the Godiva famed for riding naked through the streets of Coventry, or Godalming for that matter! This theory appears to have been preserved in names such as 'The Priory' in Church Street but there are no facts to support it nor even the existence of a priory. The dating of the first Godalming settlement is also based mainly on theory. Until recently it was always considered that the 'Ingas' element in a placename denoted an early Saxon settlement, possible of the 6th century. However, recent research which attempted to correlate the dating and distribution of pagan Saxon burial sites with that of 'ing' placenames, proposed a somewhat later date for such places.

One thing which is certain is that the Manor of Godalming was already well established by the date of its first documentary 'appearance' in the will of King Alfred the Great of Wessex. It can be said that Alfred laid the foundations of the English nation of today. He united large areas of the country against the common enemy, the Danes, and laid the basis for our legal system, drawing not only on existing laws but by making much of a fundamental nature of his own. His laws included provisions to protect weaker members of the community against oppression which now constitutes the basic principle of every democracy in the world. Alfred died on 26th October 899 and in his will he left the Manor of Godalming to his nephew, Ethelwald.

The Manor at this time covered a much larger area than the present town and stretched from Artington in the north to Haslemere in the south. Events were soon to show that Ethelwald possessed little of the wisdom or courage of his uncle. Soon after Edward the Elder's accession to the throne following Alfred's death, he rebelled and forcibly occupied the royal estates of Wimborne and Christchurch. He prepared for a siege at Wimborne but fled as soon as Edward occupied Badbury Rings near the town. Ethelwald turned traitor and joined the Danes in Northumbria and in 902 he persuaded the Danes of East Anglia to mount a raid on Mercia and Northern Wessex. It was during reprisal raids by Edward that Ethelwald was killed in battle, and his lands reverted to the King.

Godalming is not mentioned again in surviving documents until the post-conquest Domesday Book of King William I. Fortunately this comprehensive survey of England, undertaken in 1086, gives enough details to enable certain conclusions to be reached concerning Godalming during the two centuries before its compilation. Probably at some time during the 10th century, Godalming had become the meeting place of a local administrative unit known as a hundred. The hundred had its own court which usually met once a month and was presided over by the hundred reeve who acted on behalf of the King. There are a number of theories as to the origin of the hundred, one being that it consisted of ten tithings with each tithing originally being made up of ten men who stood security for each other. Each tithing was represented at the hundred court by a tithingman elected from their number. The court considered criminal matters, for example, and it also levied taxes. The Hundred of Godalming seems to have covered much the same area as the original Manor of Godalming. However, by 1086 the Manor had become split up as various parcels of land were given by successive kings to their followers. For example, Farncombe, Hurtmore, Peper Harow and Witley among others were listed separately in the Domesday Book but places such as Chiddingfold and Haslemere were not, as they still formed part of the Godalming Manor. Such omissions may also show that these settlements did not exist as such in 1086. The Manor did not even include all the area covered by the present town as part of it came into the Rectory Manor or Deanshold as it later became known.

What other evidence do we have for Saxon Godalming? Saxon pottery has been discovered at various places in the town including Bridge Street,

A reconstruction of Godalming Church in late Saxon times drawn by Samuel Welman, borough surveyor from 1872 to 1897.

This well known view of Godalming church has changed very little since 1854, the date of this engraving.

Angel Court and the Vicarage Garden. Two blocked Saxon windows in the church were discovered by Samuel Welman in the 1890s and would have originally lit the nave of the 11th century church. Some fragmentary carved stones have been attributed to the ninth century and may represent rubble from a much earlier church which occupied the same site. These stones are now displayed inside the church. The present church is a fascinating aggregation of building from the eleventh to the twentieth century. Its history has been very well covered by the excellent guide written by Alan Bott which was published in 1987, to which the present writer refers the reader for further information.

The church of Godalming, dedicated to St. Peter and St. Paul, formed in 1086 part of the holdings of one Rannulf Flambard, of whom we will say more in the next chapter. Rannulf held a second church near Tuesley which, according to the Inventory of William de Wanda written in 1220, was the first church in Godalming. This church was dedicated to the Blessed Virgin but was largely disused by 1220, as it is recorded that celebrations were held there only three times a year. In 1550 it was given to Laurence Eliot as a chapel by Edward VI. The site of the church, which is also recorded as an ancient burial ground, was excavated in the 1860s. The foundations of a chancel and nave were discovered and a total of eleven skeletons were found buried within the walls. It cannot be disputed that this church was of an early date but a careful scientific re-excavation may be the only means of determining its exact relationship to the settlement of Godalming.

Thanks to the thoroughness of the Domesday Survey it is possible to see in some detail the manorial structure of Godalming. The two manors recorded so faithfully by King William's clerks, just twenty years after the Norman conquest, were to remain a factor in the town's history until well into the 19th century.

This view of Hatch Mill in Mill Lane was sketched by William Hyde in 1913. The mill probably occupies the site of one of the three mills of Godalming Manor listed in the Domesday Book in 1086.

The Medieval Town

The medieval period was in the main a time of great prosperity and growth for the town of Godalming. It was in the wool trade and its related clothmaking industries that England's wealth was founded and Godalming contributed its share to that wealth. The countryside around the town was ideal for the rearing of sheep, and even as late as 1911 a survey of the agriculture and soils of Kent, Surrey and Sussex described the soils of the Wey Valley west of Godalming as '...too hot and dry for sheep in Summer, but stands folding admirably, and the whole system of farming centres around the sheep'.

The history of Godalming during this period is inseparable from the development of its two manors, the King's Manor and the Rectory Manor or Deanshold, both of which were briefly referred to in the previous chapter. There are many problems in the tracing of their histories, not the least is the lack of documentary evidence. A further complication is that the medieval manor was not necessarily just one parcel of land but often consisted of a number of scattered holdings. Much more research would be required to unravel the story of the two manors of Godalming and therefore only an outline is possible here.

The Domesday Survey of 1086 gave the size of the Godalming or King's Manor as 24 hides. The hide was not a fixed measurement of area but was originally calculated as the amount of land which could be worked by one plough in a year and support one family. Thus its size varied between about 60 and 180 acres, depending upon the quality of the soil. Domesday also recorded 25 acres of meadows, woodlands capable of supporting 100 pigs and a population of 50 villeins, 29 bordars and two slaves. Villeins and bordars were two classes of worker tied to the land. The population was considerably greater than this, as workers' families were not included in the list. Three mills are also recorded which is of great interest as they were later to play an important part in the growth of the town's industries but, at this time, they would undoubtedly have been corn mills. The exact location of these three mills is not recorded but the mills at Catteshall, Westbrook and Eashing, all on the River Wey, have been suggested by other writers. However any of the four mills on the little River Ock – Hatch, Ockford, Rake and Enton – must be considered as possible sites for at least one of the mills. The River Ock is small, fast flowing but has a good head of water both in summer and winter, making it ideal for driving a mill wheel. Also, the engineering problems of constructing a mill along its lower reaches would have been far less than on the River Wey. In 1086 the Manor of Godalming included tracts of land both to the north and south of the town but the process of fragmentation, begun before this date, continued throughout the next 250 years. Various parcels of land were separated from the manor and these included Catteshall and Westbrook for example.

The Manor remained a possession of the Crown until Henry III granted it to the Bishop of Salisbury in 1221. The Victoria County History of Surrey makes reference to the fact that the manor may have been granted to Stephen de Turnham in 1206. On 24th May 1224 Stephen's heirs conveyed all their rights in the Hundred and Manor of Godalming, except property in Artington and Catteshall, to the Bishop and church of Salisbury. It remained in the hands of the Bishops of Salisbury until 1541 when it was conveyed to Thomas Paston. It seems likely that he was merely an agent working for King Henry VIII, for on 20th April 1542 Paston conveyed the manor to the crown. It remained Crown property through the reigns of Edward VI, Mary and Elizabeth I. On 3rd November 1601 Elizabeth granted the Manor and Hundred to Sir George More of Loseley for the sum of £1341 8s 2¾d. One wonders what the 2¾d purchased! The manor remained in the ownership of this family until 1871.

The second Godalming Manor, The Rectory Manor or Deanshold, has

Loseley House, seat of Sir George More, who purchased the Manor of Godalming in 1601.

a slightly more complex history certainly during the medieval period. In 1086, at the time of the Domesday Survey, Rannulf Flambard held Godalming church to which belonged three hides, 15 acres of meadow and woodland for three pigs. He also held the second church near Tuesley mentioned in chapter one. Domesday also recorded that at the time of King Edward the Confessor Ulmaer held Godalming church and its land. Unfortunately nothing further is known about Ulmaer's activities in Godalming but the life of Rannulf Flambard is well documented.

Rannulf was born in Normandy and as a young man attached himself to the court of William the Conquerer. It is said that he rose through the ranks by pushing his way with flattery, treachery and 'course indulgences'. He was obviously successful as at some time during the twenty years following the Conquest, William granted him lands including those in Godalming.

Rannulf became feared by many as a spy of the King but it was during the reign of William II or William Rufus as he was known, that Rannulf achieved a position of real power in the land. Some writers have described him as justiciar to the King although his exact official position does not seem to have been defined. His main occupation was to supply the King with money and he was thoroughly unscrupulous in the way he went about it. He invariably managed to line his own pocket as well as the King's. William Rufus's reign was described by one chronicler as days when 'almost all justice slept and money was lord'. Rannulf no doubt viewed his lands in Godalming as just another source of income. The hatred for Rannulf finally showed itself in a plot to kill him. He was lured onto a ship which sailed away to 'dispose' of him but, during three days at sea, while his enemies argued over the most appropriate way of killing him, Rannulf managed to bribe the crew and secure his release. He returned to London an even greater favourite of the King than ever and in 1099 William Rufus named him Bishop of Durham. Unfortunately for Rannulf, just at the height of his power, William Rufus was killed by Walter Tirel's arrow while hunting in the New Forest and the new King, Henry I, had Rannulf flung into the Tower. He managed to escape down a rope which had been smuggled to him in a wine cask and he fled to Normandy.

Eventually Henry came to appreciate Rannulf's skills, pardoned him and restored him to the See of Durham. He also regained possession of his lands in Godalming at this time but Henry granted them along with the church of Heytesbury, Wiltshire, to the cathedral church of St Mary, Salisbury, as a prebend that Rannulf could enjoy until his death. In his later years it appears that Rannulf became a somewhat reformed character and he devoted much of his time to the organisation of building works, especially at Durham. Certain early twelfth century works in

Godalming Church may also belong to this period. Rannulf died in 1128 but the Salisbury claim to his Godalming estates was not finally confirmed until about 1157. Rannulf's holdings in Godalming and Tuesley eventually passed to the Dean and Chapter of Salisbury and became known as the Rectory Manor or Deanshold. Therefore, after 1221, both manors of Godalming came under the lordship of Salisbury but with different landlords. The Dean of Salisbury held the Rectory Manor and the Bishop of Salisbury the Manor of Godalming. This apparent technicality of ownership was to have a markedly different effect upon the histories of the two manors through the next seven hundred years.

It has already been briefly mentioned that the Manor of Godalming passed from the Bishop of Salisbury to Henry VIII via Thomas Paston in 1542 and then into private hands in 1601. In contrast, the Rectory Manor remained, apart from the period of the Commonwealth, the property of the Dean and Chapter until 1846. Its history during this period is one of a complicated series of leases and sub-leases. On more than one occasion this leasing, coupled with various exchanges by the lease-holders to consolidate their lands, resulted in the Dean and Chapter almost losing sight of their freehold. In 1622 the Dean had to take proceedings in Chancery against Valentine Castillion, the lessee at the time, in order to confirm his rights as Lord of the Manor.

The Castillion family were the main tenants until the beginning of the 18th century. John Baptist Castillion was responsible for the rebuilding of the Parsonage House or Rectory in the 1580s. This house, which stood on land between the church and the River Wey now occupied by the Phillips Memorial Garden and Cloister, replaced an earlier house of some magnificence. In the first decades of the 16th century it was described as having 'a porch arched over with stone, a great and little gate covered with tiles and stabling for many horses'. The Castillion house which replaced it survived until the early 1860s, by which time it had become something of a slum divided into tenements. Fortunately a good photograph of it survives to show what a substantial place it was. It cannot have been a particularly healthy abode considering its proximity to the river.

During the 18th century the Rectory manor was in the possession of the Oglethorpes of Westbrook including General James Oglethorpe, the founder of the State of Georgia. The manor was vested in the Ecclesiastical Commissioners in 1846 and when they finally gained possession in about 1861 the land was sold off. The name of the manor still survives in buildings and places which were once within its bounds. Until the latter half of the 19th century there was a Deanery Farm at the bottom of Charterhouse Hill and its barn still survives as the local scout hut. The road which ran past the farm was called Sandy Lane and was not renamed

The parish church and Parsonage House or Rectory from Boarden Bridge, photographed about 1860. The house was built by John Baptist Castillion in the 1580s, replacing an earlier building of some considerable substance which stood on the same site between the church and river. The Castillion house had been demolished by 1865.

Charterhouse Road until some years after the coming of the school in 1872. Deanery Place, opposite the church in Church Street, and Dean Road, also preserve the name.

Despite the markedly different histories of the two manors of Godalming, the town itself seems to have happily retained a corporate identity. This is doubtless because, as a tithing of Godalming Hundred, its representative at the Hundred Court, the tithingman, spoke for the town as a whole. Godalming's first recorded charter was granted by Edward I to the Bishop of Salisbury on 7th June 1300. This charter, although granted for the Godalming Manor, would have materially affected the prosperity of the whole town, as it granted a market each Monday and a fair on the vigil, the feast and the morrow of St Peter and St Paul. Similar charters for other towns in England gave the impetus for expansion or indeed the foundation of a town. In Godalming's case it is very probable that the basic street plan was already in existence by 1300. Recent excavations have uncovered 12th and 13th century pottery not only in The Mint and Mint Street area but also in Bridge Street at the other end of the town.

The granting of a market may be taken to imply that Godalming's future growth was as a market town but this is far from the truth. In this role it was always to be overshadowed by its big neighbour to the north, Guildford. Godalming's development was based on its industries of cloth-making, framework knitting, paper-making, tanning and leatherwork. As the importance of these industries grew, so families of entrepreneurs prospered. These families came increasingly to hold the real power in the town as that of the manorial lord declined. By the second half of the 16th century, it was local men like the Elyots, the Castillions and the Perriors who saw the advantages to be gained by persuading Queen Elizabeth to grant the town a charter of incorporation which would further increase their influence in the town's affairs.

The arms of the Borough of Godalming—although the town was granted borough status by Elizabeth I in 1575, it did not acquire an official coat of arms until 1893.

The Borough through Three Centuries

'The Queene to all to whom etc. Greeting, Whereas the Inhabitants of the Town of Godallminge in our County of Surry being in moste extreme ruine and decay have humbly beseeched us ... to creat erect and make the inhabitants of the said aforesaid Towne into a body Corporate and pollitiq ...' These opening lines of the charter of Queen Elizabeth I for the incorporation of Godalming are a seventeenth century translation of the original Latin charter which appears to have been lost long ago. The reference to the town being 'in moste extreme ruine and decay' seems only to have been the legal jargon of the day as Godalming was most certainly a prosperous place at this time. In 1563 it had been designated a market town by statute and its cloth trade was thriving. The charter was dated 25th January 1574 but New Year's Day occurred on March 25th until the calendar was changed in 1752. Therefore, calculated on our modern calendar the date of the Godalming charter would be 25th January 1575. In the charter it was stipulated that the townspeople should meet every feast of St. Michael to choose a principal inhabitant to be warden for a year and the charter named John Perrior 'an approved man and an Inhabitant of the said Towne of Godallming to be ye first and modern warden of the said Towne ...'.

John Perrior, Perior or Peryer came from a family who had for some time held lands on the Surrey/Sussex borders and it is probable that as a child he lived at Wisborough Green. It appears that he came to Godalming where the family also had property, in the early 1540s. A deed of 20th January 1529 refers to the croft of John Peryer called 'Le Barton' as being the southern boundary of a messuage and garden which formed part of what is now the Mint in Mill Lane. The John of 1529 may have been the father of the first warden but it is likely that he did not actually live at 'Le Barton' at this time but was still an inhabitant of Wisborough. John Peryer Senior died on 25th March 1543 and his son John inherited his holdings in Godalming and soon after moved to the town. From this time his name appears regularly in various local documents as one obviously playing a major part in local affairs. He also became one of the town's wealthiest inhabitants and a natural candidate for the important position of the town's first warden. In his later years he lived in a house set back from the road at the southern end of the High Street. This part of the street leading to Ockford was at that time unpaved and for obvious reasons called Sand Street. He died in June 1599 and was buried in the churchyard on 19th June. His bequests in his will, written shortly before he died, included a dyehouse and a red cow with a white face. The reference to the dyehouse is good evidence of the source of at least some of his wealth and was left to his son, John. The cow, which seems almost to have been a family pet, became the property of his daughter.

The charter of 1575 also granted the town a weekly market to be held on a Wednesday and thereby Queen Elizabeth gave up her rights, held as Lord of the Manor, to the market first granted under the charter of 1300. The new market continued to be held on a Wednesday until 1674 when it changed to a Friday but it had returned to being held according to the Elizabethan charter by the early nineteenth century. A fair to last three days on the eve, the day and the morrow of the feast of the Purification of the Blessed Virgin Mary was also granted but the original fair, held by the lord of the manor, continued to take place. The warden or a deputy was empowered to collect the tolls from the market and the fair, which in effect were the equivalent of modern rates. The market, which was mainly for corn, declined in importance during the nineteenth century and finally ceased about 1879. The fairs continued in one form or another through the nineteenth century, although by this time they had become reduced to one day each, February 13th and July 10th. The February fair

This end of the High Street, seen here about 1905, was at one time called Sand Street.

The old Market House from an engraving which appeared in *The Gentleman's Magazine* in the year it was demolished, 1814. Its unique replacement is undoubtedly the town's most famous landmark but Godhelmians are still divided as to whether it should be called the 'Pepperpot' or 'Pepperbox'.

was still recorded in the local directory as late as 1910, but the July fair, which was the original granted to the Lord of the Manor in 1300, ceased about 1870.

The market and probably the fair as well were sited on that triangle of land at the south western end of the High Street where the old Town Hall, known affectionately as the Pepperbox or Pepperpot, now stands. In medieval times this area would have been considerably larger than it is now but successive building on adjacent sites through the centuries has seriously reduced its size by encroachment. Each time a property was rebuilt or refronted the owner took the opportunity to steal an extra foot or two on the front and he invariably got away with it. It is probable that this small area of the town, where Church Street meets the High Street, has been the seat of local administration for over a thousand years. The first Saxon moots, an early form of court, may have been convened here and certainly by the end of the tenth century, the court of Godalming Hundred would have met here. During the medieval period it also became the place where the manorial courts of the Godalming Manor were conducted.

At some time in the late medieval period a building was constructed in the middle of the market place in which to conduct local administrative affairs. The present building which dates from 1814, was a replacement for an earlier Hundred House which was in existence by 1532. A deed of that year refers to the King's Way which led from the Hundred House towards the East Bridge, the King's Way being the present High Street and East Bridge the Town Bridge. This building naturally became the seat from which the Warden conducted his business and also became known as the Market House. Records show that by 1616 it was in a poor state of repair; in the will of John Purchase, a dyer of Godalming, dated 25th May of that year, he left money for very major renovations including 'timber worke, ground pynning, walling, and other necessary reparations ....'. Later Warden Accounts regularly include entries for further repairs but, by the late eighteenth century, plans were put forward to build a new market house because the original was literally falling down. However, it struggled on for another twenty years or so and was finally demolished to make way for the present building in 1814. The money to pay for the new building was raised by public subscription which amounted to £783 7s 2d and a further £81 19s 6d was raised by selling materials from the old Hundred House. This seems a remarkably large sum considering how decayed it was supposed to be. The subscribers included a number of the

The Pepperbox in 1903, with Henry Craddock's 'hidden' shop to the right.

leading local worthies; the Lord of the Manor gave £50 and William Gill of Eashing House, £80.

Skilled local architect, John Perry, drafted the plans for a simple building which has since become the very essence of the town. Without it a great deal of the town's character and individuality would be lost and few present Godhelmians would ever consider its removal. The building has not always been thought of in this way for in the late nineteenth century there were several campaigns to have it removed. One of the leading campaigners was H.T. Craddock who ran a business as a stationer and printer in premises close to the Pepperbox; the firm still continues in Great George Street to this day. Mr Craddock seems to have been obsessed with the idea that trade would improve if his shop were no longer hidden behind the old and redundant building. An advertisement in the Godalming Almanac and Directory for 1898 reads: 'LOST!! behind the Town Hall, Godalming. H.T. Craddock hopes that in a short time his printing office will be easily FOUND! when the old "Pepper Box" is cleared away and we have an open space instead of an obstruction in the centre of the High Street, and suitable Municipal Buildings and Entertainment Hall erected for "plucky little Godalming" '. Mr Craddock published the Directory for many years for which any researcher of the town's history will be forever grateful. Most townspeople will also be forever grateful that, although new municipal buildings were opened in Bridge Street in 1908, our worthy printer and publisher was not totally successful with his campaign.

Just as H.T. Craddock represented the successful Godalming businessman of the nineteenth century, so did the likes of John Perrior, our first warden, represent those of the sixteenth century. The fortunes of families like the Perriors were founded or grew on the wool trade or the manufacture of cloth and some members of these families became prominent figures nationally. The Champions, for example, became leading merchants in London, Richard Champion was knighted and also served as Lord Mayor of the City in 1565. Richard Wyatt was a London merchant whose country home was at Hall Place, Shackleford. He also held property in Chiddingfold, Compton, Hambledon and an ironworks at Dunsfold. When he died on 3rd December 1619 he left money for the establishment of an 'Oyspitall' or almshouse for the benefit of 'ten poore menn', five from Godalming, two from Puttenham and one each from Compton, Dunsfold and Hambledon. Wyatt's Almshouses still stand near the main road on the north east outskirts of the town. A large number of other buildings of the sixteenth century also survive in Godalming as further evidence of the general prosperity of the town at this time.

Little is known of the government of the town for the forty years or so after the 1575 charter. No record of the wardens has survived nor indeed any details of how they actually went about their business. The names of some of the wardens have been traced from other documentary sources such as the Parish Register and included William Perior in 1606. He was no doubt related to the first warden. However, it is clear that the system of government was not entirely satisfactory for in 1620 it proved necessary to issue a further document to regularise the town's administration. This document was entitled 'Ordinances and constitutions made and established for the better order and government of the Town of Godalming in the County of Surry (sic)'. They were signed by the Right Hon. Francis Lord Verulam who was Lord Chancellor of England at that time. In all there were twenty-seven ordinances which ranged from the election of the warden and the appointment of officers such as the bailiff, to restrictions to prevent the inhabitants spending more than half an hour at a time in the local hostelry. These ordinances also contain the first recorded reference to the election of 'eight of the gravest and fittest men of the Inhabitants of the said Town to be his (the Warden's) Assistants'. Every year the Warden was to be chosen from three of the assistants nominated by the out-going Warden. The assistants were elected for life and therefore the administration soon developed into a self-perpetuating club. There was ample opportunity for corruption although there is no

Richard Wyatt and his family—from a brass in the chapel of his almshouses.

evidence that this ever became a really serious problem. However, many of the wardens kept no account of expenditure or income and pocketed any profits, pleading that they had made a personal loss while in office.

The money from the market and fair tolls and fines for infringements of the ordinances were used for paying expenses. These included items such as repairs to the town clock and the Market House, and the bellman's salary. In 1761-2 it was recorded that £5 5s 11d was paid to William Peto, carpenter, for repairs to the town's two fire engines. On the three recorded occasions when the fire engines were used during the year, the firemen were given a total of 12s 6d worth of beer by way of assistance. As another source of income the Warden could make an assessment which would be collected from the inhabitants by the town bailiff. Such assessments were called 'voluntary subscriptions' in the accounts. It is interesting to note that the Warden often made an assessment despite having tolls which more than covered expenditure. Most of the Wardens who failed to keep accounts no doubt kept such profits to themselves.

In 1620 no inhabitant of Godalming could afford to miss any such chance to make a profit for these were hard times for the town and Surrey in general. The reasons are manifold but at a local level it was the decline in the cloth trade which was the major cause. The cloth workers of the neighbouring town of Guildford fared even worse than those of Godalming and as early as 1614 the Archbishop of Canterbury, George Abbot, who had been born in Guildford, was providing money for schemes to alleviate Guildford's problems. The languishing cloth trade in Guildford and Wonersh has been attributed to the dishonest practice of over-stretching the material. The purchaser would presumably discover that he had been cheated the first time it was washed. The truth is, as usual, not quite so simple but another factor was that the native cloth was simply no longer fashionable. In 1630 local magistrates were instructed to make collections for the benefit of the unemployed cloth workers of Godalming. Despite its problems Godalming fared better than most, a fact illustrated by the ship money assessment of 1636. The money was needed to pay for ships to fight the Dutch and Godalming's contribution amounted to £90. This compared with Farnham at £94, Reigate at £60 and Guildford at only £53.

This period of depression in the seventeenth century corresponded with a marked increase in non-conformity in religion in Godalming. By the end of the century both Quakers and Non-conformists were well established in the town. It is recorded in 1669 that conventicles, held every Sunday at Westbrook by John Platt, the ejected minister of West Horsley, were attended by seven or eight hundred people. Another monthly conventicle held at the house of Quaker, Henry Gill, is said to have attracted four or five hundred. These figures may be an exaggeration but they do represent a substantial movement away from the established church. In the 1640s even the ministers of the church were under fire from their parishioners, and in 1643 this culminated in the ejection of the vicar, Nicholas Andrewes. He was accused by a number of his flock of a variety of misdemeanors including that he was a 'haunter and frequenter of tiplings in Innes and Tavernes' and that he had numerous crucifixes and 'Romish' pictures hanging in his Vicarage. Poor Nicholas was imprisioned and eventually died from the effects of his ill-treatment. Of course his problems counted for little compared with those that the country as a whole was facing at this time.

Godalming cannot claim any great battles or engagements during the Civil War and for the crucial years of the fighting between the King and

Godalming's High Street is, of course, not as wide and spacious as shown in this engraving of 1870. However, many of the buildings depicted, such as the King's Arms Royal Hotel, are still instantly recognisable today.

Parliament the town was dominated by the activities at Farnham which Waller held for Parliament.

After the Restoration, Godalming's fortunes turned for the better. Portsmouth began to grow in importance as a naval port and Godalming conveniently found itself on the main route to that town. Throughout the eighteenth century coaching inns flourished and these included the 'Great George', the building of which still stands on the corner of Great George Street but has been converted into shops. A glance up above the shop fronts will show that the impressive Georgian front of the inn survives. Other inns included the 'White Hart' which, as the 'Antelope', had been an inn since the sixteenth century. The imposing timber-framed building survives as shops opposite the old Town Hall. The most well known of Godalming's coaching inns is 'The King's Arms' and it is there in 1698 that it received a most distinguished guest, Czar Peter the Great of Russia, and his entourage. Peter was returning from Portsmouth where he had been viewing ships of the English Navy when he stopped at the famous inn run by James Moon. The landlord soon came to regret the Russians' choice of lodgings for they proceeded to consume vast quantities of food and drink with little thought of actually paying for it. A contemporary list of the contents of this gastronomic orgy is preserved in the Bodleian Library at Oxford. It goes without saying that no Godalming wench was safe during their short stay. They departed to the house of John Evelyn, the famous diarist, at Deptford, where they stayed three months. Evelyn's bailiff later described the royal party very succinctly as 'right nasty' and Evelyn himself recorded in his diary that they did £150 worth of damage to the house and its garden, an enormous sum in those days.

The increasing need for mobility in the eighteenth century led to the establishment of turnpike roads throughout the country. The Turnpike Trust charged tolls to travellers and in return was supposed to keep the roads in good repair. The toll cottage in Ockford Road still stands and here a gate across the road would have prevented traffic from passing in or out of the town without payment. The tollgate was originally north of the town but was moved in 1767 after the opening of the Godalming Navigation. The Turnpike Trust realised that they were losing tolls on goods brought by road from the south which were then loaded onto barges at the Wharf. The tollgate was re-sited yet again in 1855, when the railway was built along the valley of the River Ock.

The need to improve the road through the town was also reflected in the rebuilding of the town bridge in 1782 as a county bridge open to all traffic. The previous bridge had belonged to the Lord of the Manor and was only opened in times of flood. At other times traffic crossed the river by the adjacent ford. The river could also be forded at the other end of the town by the church. Pedestrians crossed here using Bolden or Boarden

The Town Bridge about 1900 – at this time small craft could be moored immediately downstream of the bridge. Both Bridge House on the extreme left and the spire of the Congregational Church survived until the 1960s. In 1930 the bridge was widened on the downstream side to help prevent further accidents such as that which befell a well known local octogenarian, Mr. J. Gorringe, who in 1926 was crushed to death against the parapet of the bridge by a passing timber truck.

Bridge but Borough Road Bridge was not built until 1874.

In the spring of 1764 the Godalming Navigation was opened from Guildford and for the first time the town was linked to the main canal network of England. This provided a great boost to several of the town's trades and industries. The town wharf, just downstream from the bridge, became a thriving centre for the shipment of bulk goods, especially timber, corn and stone.

This then was the bustling town watched over by the Warden and his eight assistants, a town whose fortunes were based on its industries of framework knitting, tanning, leatherwork, paper-making and stone quarrying. The old industry of cloth-making which had done so much to establish the town in the medieval period, still continued, though on a much reduced scale, but its significance had not been forgotten. The town seal applied to all official documents still carried as its central motif the representation of the woolpack.

The Parish Church and Boarden Bridge as seen from the Lammas Lands before the construction of the railway embankment in 1858 and Borough Road in 1874.

The town seal of 1749—the original is in the town museum.

THE STOCKING FRAME

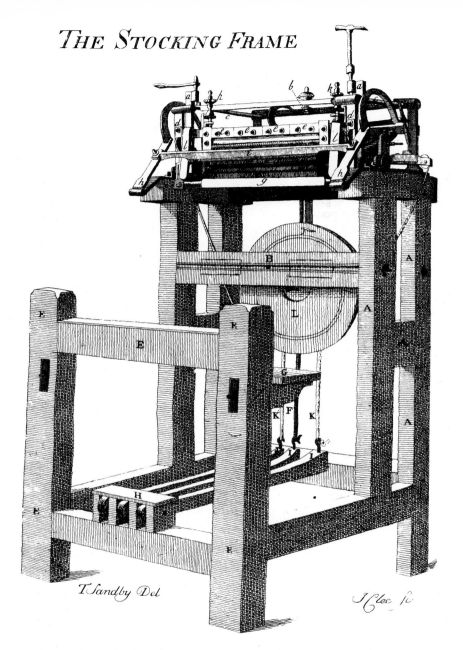

An eighteenth century engraving of a knitting frame. A similar frame of slightly later date is displayed in Godalming Museum.

Industries and Trades

It is not known exactly when the wool trade and its related industries became established in West Surrey but the natural advantages of the area must have been apparent from early medieval times. The hills around Godalming, with their light loamy soils, were considered highly suitable for the folding of sheep and the adjacent countryside, especially the chalk downs, offered good grass upon which the animal thrived. The rivers and streams provided a good head of water to drive the fulling mills, fulling being an important process in the manufacture of cloth and a few miles away were major deposits of fuller's earth, a substance essential to that process.

The manufacture of woollen cloth was certainly well established in the area by 1252 as it is recorded that 'Chalons of Guildford' were bought for King Henry III at Winchester Fair in that year. 'Chalons' were a type of cloth named after Chalons-sur-Marne in France. In 1391 Guildford is mentioned in a Parliamentary Statute, a well known translation of which reads: 'that......of old time divers cloths were made in the town of Guildford and other places within the Counties of Surrey, Sussex and Southampton, called "Cloths of Guildford" which were of good making and of good value, and did bear a great name'. Godalming was certainly one of the 'other places' included in this Statute and by this time the town was already economically dependent on the sheep and its wool. As early as 1339 it was recorded at the Godalming Hundred Court for example that 30 sheep were offered as bail. The processes required to turn raw wool into the finished product of coloured cloth were very labour intensive and it is likely that a large proportion of the town's population was involved in the industry.

After the initial sorting of the wool, the carding, combing and spinning would be the home employment of the women but the most important of the processes, that of weaving, was probably undertaken entirely by men. The cloth thus produced was still in a raw oily state and the next operation, fulling, cleansed and thickened it in a mixture of water and fuller's earth. Fuller's earth occurs as a natural substance in geological deposits of Lower Cretaceous age, especially at Nutfield near Reigate. In medieval times it was considered so valuable that its export was forbidden and, until recently, it was extensively dug in the area. During fulling the earth absorbed the oils from the wool, the process being originally carried out by men trampling the cloth in a trough and known as 'walking'. It is from this source that the common surname 'Walker' is derived. Some time during the thirteenth century the process became mechanised with the introduction of 'the stocks', an instrument consisting of an upright to which was hinged a wooden bar called a 'perch'. The cloth was beaten with the end of the perch which soon came to be driven by water power and thus the fulling mill came into being. Several of Godalming's mills served as fulling mills at some time during their long histories. During the fourteenth century a fulling mill was constructed adjacent to the cornmill at Catteshall and Rake Mill near Milford is recorded as a fulling mill in 1577.

The fulled cloth was now stretched and dried on racks or tenters. This stretching on tenters has left its legacy in the English language with the phrase 'to be on tenterhooks'. John Perrior, grandson of the first Warden of the town, died in 1632 and bequests to his son included 'all his followers and boords and the upper racke in Barton'. Barton, as mentioned in the previous chapter, was adjacent to The Mint but there were undoubtedly many other racks in the town. The use of the tenter led to the abuse of over-stretching the cloth and there are many recorded cases of Surrey clothiers being accused of this offence. In 1565 twelve Godalming clothiers were thus accused of using various instruments to strain and stretch their cloth.

After fulling and drying the cloth was passed to a worker called a rower whose job was to draw up all the loose fibres from the cloth by combing it with teazles. Presumably the teazles were gathered locally either from the wild or cultivated. From the rower the cloth came to the shearman who cut off the fibres which had been raised by the teazles. The finished surface of the cloth depended entirely upon his skill with the shears and much human endeavour could come to nought with one careless snip.

The cloth was now ready for the dyer. A variety of different coloured dyes were available but in the Godalming area, certainly by the sixteenth century, much of the cloth was given a blue colour, from a dye made from woad. Most of the woad used in the medieval cloth industry of England was imported and Southampton became the centre of the trade in the plant. John Aubrey writing in the late seventeenth century said of Godalming: 'here they make mix'd Kersies and blue Kersies for the Canaries, which for their Colour are not equall'd by any in England'. The name Kersey was derived from the place of that name in Suffolk but Hampshire (or Southamptonshire to give it its full name) and south-west Surrey became one of the most important centres for their production. These Kersies even came to be known as 'Hampshire Kersies'. Aubrey's reference to the Canary Islands as the destination of Godalming's cloth is slightly curious but the islands in the Atlantic may have operated as a distribution centre for various markets in foreign lands. There were a number of dyehouses in Godalming and by the sixteenth century they may have been using locally grown woad. In 1685 John Woods of Godalming 'devised to his kinsman John Woods his messuage and dyehouse with vats, furnaces and all other implements and things belonging to the dyehouse trade and dyehouse.....'. John Woods represented the typical clothier of Godalming who employed a number of workers to carry out the various processes described in this chapter which resulted in the finished product, a roll of cloth. In addition to the dyehouse given to the second John Woods he also devised 'his shears and shearing boards, cloth press and parchment for pressing of cloth, and all his racks for drying of cloth and all other his implements and tools used about his shearing trade'.

Mention has already been made of the decline of the cloth industry at the beginning of the seventeenth century but in Godalming it seemed to weather the storm far better than in adjacent Guildford, Farnham and Wonersh. By the end of the seventeenth century the industry seems to have died out completely in Farnham and Wonersh at a time when Aubrey was writing of Godalming 'this town is eminent for clothing, the most of any place in this County'. The town's importance to the trade in the previous century had been emphasized by its specific mention in a Statute of 1557/58 and it is worth repeating the relevant section in full: 'Provided always that it shall be lawful to all and every person or persons which now do, or hereafter shall inhabit or dwell in any of the Shires North Wales, or South Wales, Cheshire, Lancashire, Westmoreland, Cumberland, Northumberland, the Bishoprick of Durham, Cornwall, Suffolk, Kent, the Town of Goddelmine in the County of Surrey, or Yorkshire being not within twelve miles of the citie of York, or in any of the towns or villages near adjoining the water of the Stroud in the County of Gloucester, where clothes have been usually made by the spate of twenty years last past....'. The manufacture of cloth continued on an ever decreasing scale in the town until the middle of the last century when a few Kersies were still being made.

The decline of the cloth industry did not mean a similar decline in the industrial fortunes of Godalming. As cloth fell from importance it was replaced by the framework knitting of hosiery and this resilient town became a major centre for the production of stockings, in wool, silk and later also in cotton. The framework industry had its origins in the invention by William Lee in 1589 of a frame using woollen yarn. He applied to Queen Elizabeth for a patent but was turned down, the Queen commenting that 'had Mr. Lee made a machine that would have made silk stockings, I should, I think, have been somewhat justified in granting him a patent for that monopoly....'. Lee and his brother, James, took the invention to France but, shortly after 1610, James returned and set up frames in London. From there use of the improved frame, knitting mainly in silk, had spread to Godalming by the 1660s.

In the early eighteenth century use of the frame was well established as the staple industry of the town. Many of those involved in the trade worked from their homes and one of their characteristic brick-fronted cottages still survives in Mint Street, opposite the garden of the Rose and Crown. They are three storeys high with a long window just below the eaves, and at this window the knitter would work from dawn to dusk, making the most use of all available light. Other workers were employed in small factories like that which belonged to Elizabeth Marshall. In her will, dated 1823, she left forty-three stocking frames in her stocking shop. The long hours toiling at the frame brought small financial rewards for the knitters and in 1778-79 there were petitions to Parliament for a Bill to establish a minimum weekly wage of six shillings. At the time the wage could amount to as little as four shillings and sixpence but the petitions which included one from Godalming, failed. Earlier in the century a Framework Knitters Company had been founded but the knitters of Godalming found its restrictive practices not to their liking and in 1753 they successfully petitioned Parliament against the imposition of the Company's byelaws.

A major development in the hosiery industry was the granting in 1788 of a patent to George Holland of Bloomsbury for the manufacture, from

The results of a fire at the Oak Bark Tannery, Mill Lane, on 7th March 1905.

specially prepared wool, of 'Fleecy and Segovia Hosiery'. Holland set up a factory in Godalming, the works moving about 1845 to the Langham site later occupied by the Godalming Laundry. His patent specification described a 'new invented method of making stockings, gloves, mitts, socks, caps, coats, waistcoats, breeches, cloaks, and other clothing, and linings for the same, for persons afflicted with gout, rheumatism, and other complaints requiring warmth, and of common use in cold climates, and of making false or downy calves in stockings, a thing never before put in practise.' Holland's venture was extremely successful and fleecy hosiery made in the town became famous throughout the world. This success encouraged at least two other factories to start up nearby. Framework knitting as such slowly declined through the last century and became concentrated in the two or three firms mentioned above. When the firm of Allen and Solly moved to Nottingham in 1888, several local families migrated with the firm but a few still remained to carry the industry into the twentieth century. Godalming's connection with the woollen trades is continued to this day in part of the original Fleecy and Segovia Hosiery Factory in Catteshall Lane.

The River Wey and the River Ock played their part in the development of the woollen industries as source of both water and power and they were also the main factor in the growth of the town's two other major industries, leatherworking and paper making. The tanning of the hides of the ox, cow and calf required a good supply of water and an ample source of the important tanning agent, oak bark, which was readily available from the woodland areas to the south of Godalming. The industry was well established by the fifteenth century when a number of references to tanners and leatherworkers occur in the proceedings of the Manorial Court and the Hundred Court. Tanneries and leatherworks were operating at various places in the town during the next four hundred years. A tannery which stood between the River Ock and the Ockford Road opposite Ockford Mill was in existence by 1745 as a mortgage of the property of that date has survived. Westbrook Mills may also have been in use as a leather mill from about this time and leatherworking continued on the site until the early 1950s. A tannery was certainly in existence in Mill Lane by 1808 when a bark house for the grinding of the oak bark was erected in the tanyard. Other tanneries are recorded in Meadrow, Wharf Street, Brighton Road and at Catteshall Mill.

Paper-making, like leatherworking and tanning, required large quantities of water for its various processes which were carried on in the Godalming area at least from the early seventeenth century. Towards the end of that century John Aubrey, writing about Godalming paper, commented 'that in the reign of King James I coarse paper, commonly call'd whited brown Paper, was first made in England, especially in

The Oak Bark Tannery, Mill Lane, about 1902 – an image more popularly associated with the industrial north than a Surrey town like Godalming. The buildings on the extreme right still survive.

Surrey and about Windsor; and this Place, I have frequently heard, bore the Bell from all this County, for its excellence in Manufacture'. Part of Catteshall Mill was already being used as a paper mill by this time and the industry continued here until 1928. Paper was also made at Eashing Mill, which was bought by a papermaker in 1658 and was still producing paper in the 1870s.

Most of Godalming's mills have a long tradition as cornmills in addition to their use in the other industries mentioned in this chapter. However, the town had one industry which had no need of the mill as a source of power, Bargate stone quarrying. Throughout its two thousand year history as a building material, Bargate stone has always been extracted almost entirely by hand. The stone was used in the construction of the Romano-British farmstead at Binscombe, in the pre-conquest Godalming Church and for a large variety of buildings from the early medieval period on. Examples of its use are to be seen all around the Guildford and Godalming area, though it was also exported to London and even as far as Leicester. The stone occurs as large masses called 'doggers' in an otherwise soft sand, and the quarrymen developed a unique way of extracting it called 'jumping a stone'. An iron block was used as the pivot for a long crowbar which was placed under one end of the stone to be dug out. A plank was then placed at right angles on the opposite end of the crowbar. Several men, using long poles to balance themselves, then jumped up and down on the plank in unison. This process gradually loosened the 'dogger' from the quarry face. Quarrying continued until the Second World War at large quarries near Shackstead Lane, on Primrose Ridge and at the top of Eashing Lane but demand was not renewed after the war and the quarries were abandoned. The stone was also crushed for road metalling and in later years this seems to have been the mainstay of the industry. There was a stone crusher in Eashing Lane and the large quarry near the railway south of Ockford Mill had its own railway siding to facilitate the rapid transportation of the crushed stone. It is really rather fortunate for Godalming that the stone proved too soft to take the wear and tear of modern traffic or the hills surrounding the town might by now have been quarried away to satisfy the insatiable demand of the modern road builder.

Quarrymen 'jumping a stone' in Shackstead Lane Quarry about 1920.

The town from Frith Hill about 1900 – the prominent dip in the hills to the right of the church is the valley of the River Ock. Smoke from the stacks of Westbrook Leather Mills beside the River Wey drifts towards the town on a westerly breeze.

Part of late nineteenth century industrial Godalming viewed from across the railway.

Victorian Godalming

"Your carriage awaits you, sir" – outside Sidney Ballard's drapers shop in the 1880s. On the extreme left is the shop of W. Clarke and Son, grocers, who were in business here until 1888. They also had a branch in Wharf Street wherein gastronomic connoisseurs could purchase the 'noted Godalming Sausage'.

Godalming in the early nineteenth century was a bustling, thriving industrial town. The buildings fronting the main thoroughfare, from Bridge Street at one end of the town to Sand Street at the other, hid dozens of small tenements and workshops which were reached through common entrances between the shops and houses. Small yards like Harts Yard were both the homes and the workplaces of saddlers, farriers, whitesmiths, cordwainers, carpenters and the like. The census of 1811 showed that 476 out of 697 families in the parish were employed in trade, manufacturing or handicrafts. Most of these families would have been living in the town itself. The Wharf was a hive of activity as barges were loaded with goods such as timber, flour, manure, iron and oak bark destined for markets many miles away. Barges returned to unload corn for the mills, coal and a mass of lesser commodities. The High Street was

busy with coaches and wagons bringing soldiers, sailors, convicts, gentry
and admirals on route to Portsmouth. To cater for the thirst and famine of
this motley host of travellers nearly every other building in the town
seems to have become an inn or alehouse. In Bridge Street where there
are no longer any pubs at all, the visitor and bargeman could choose from
six including 'The Three Colts', 'The Row Barge' and 'Horse and
Groom'. Bridge Street had also become the brewing centre of the town
with no less than four separate breweries by the 1880s.

Convicts on their way to be transported were often housed in a special
room at the Kings Arms or the Red Lion or even in the small dungeon
attached to the Market House. In 1761 it was recorded in the Warden's
account book that 98 French prisoners were lodged in the Market House
itself and the Warden, Abraham Toft, received seventeen shillings in
payment. It was also not unusual for soldiers to store their baggage there
while they were billeted in the town.

The billeting of troops in the town's inns during the Napoleonic Wars
put the landlords under great financial strain and among petitioners for a
reduction in the number of troops was Thomas Taylor who ran 'The
George' in the High Street. This inn may at one time have been called
'The George and Dragon' but later became known as 'The Great
George', presumably when 'The Little George' opened next door but

In the early 1890s the graceful symmetry of the King's Arms had yet to be spoilt by shops.

The coaching inns of Godalming suffered a sudden decline with the opening of the railway through to Portsmouth in January 1859. A direct result of this was the insertion of shops into the ground floor frontages of inns such as the Great George and the King's Arms. The eighteenth century edifice of the Great George Inn, prominent on the right of this view of the High Street in about 1908, has survived to this day as have most of the other buildings shown here. The motorcar, just visible in the distance, was still quite a novelty in 1908 but as early as 1904 the Corporation had restricted the speed of automobiles passing through the Borough to a maximum of 10m.p.h.

one. Before about 1850 Great George Street, at the side of the inn, was still a private entrance to a property called 'Broadgate'. Similarly, South Street did not exist being only the entrance to another yard, whilst Moss Lane, a name derived from John Moth who owned property here in the sixteenth century, led only to a footpath. Queen Street was not built until 1897, the year of Queen Victoria's Diamond Jubilee, from which it derived its original name of Jubilee Street.

Despite these changes which were to take place in later years, much of the High Street and Church Street buildings of the early 1800s have survived to the present day and the general view of the town is surprisingly little altered. However, living conditions for the majority of the inhabitants have by comparison changed beyond all recognition. In the 1820s and 30s many lived in cramped and crowded tenements with no proper sanitation or adequate water supply. Cess pits were usually situated in small backyards just a few feet from the well which provided drinking water. Godalming was not a healthy place in which to live and throughout its history the population was regularly reduced by epidemics of one form or another. No doubt the town was afflicted with the Black Death in the mid-fourteenth century but, even after this first visitation of the plague had passed, the dread disease was never far away. For example it struck again in 1636 and when London suffered the Great Plague in 1665, it travelled to Godalming soon after and was at its worst from July to November 1666. On 24th July, it was recorded in the parish register: 'William Smith and his two children of ye great sickness'. Many more were to follow the poor Smith family. Smallpox was the great killer in the eighteenth century and there were several epidemics in which large numbers of the inhabitants died. The nineteenth century saw outbreaks of typhoid and cholera with similar results.

The town had originally been paved in about 1528 but in 1825 an Act was passed to establish a board of commissioners responsible for the paving, lighting and general improvement of the streets of the town. Godalming was still watched over by the Warden and his eight assistants but ten years later a Parliamentary report on the town's administration

The High Street about 1870 – the horse and cart are parked outside M. Harris's ironmongers shop. The White Hart on the right was converted to shops in 1932. This photograph along with several other excellent early pictures of the town may have been taken by Mr. G. West who established himself in Godalming as a 'photographic artist' in 1853.

considered that it was not being governed according to the ordinances of 1620 and that many of its bye-laws were illegal. The problem was soon solved when the corporation was reconstituted under the Municipal Corporations Act of 1835, and Henry Marshall became its first leader with the title of Mayor in 1836. The eight 'assistants' were replaced by four aldermen and twelve councillors whose numbers were later increased to six and eighteen respectively.

The industrial importance of Godalming was slowly declining at this time but the town was given a boost in 1849 when the railway arrived at the 'old' station on the corner of Meadrow and Chalk Road. For ten years Godalming was the terminus of the line from London. The railway was an obvious threat to the fortunes of the Godalming Navigation but in general it brought prosperity. However, when the line was extended to Havant and the existing station opened in 1859, Godalming became merely another stop on the mainline and its lucrative coaching trade ceased. The original station continued to offer a passenger and goods service until Farncombe Station was built in 1897, thereafter it exclusively handled goods traffic until closure in 1969.

The early 1860s must have been a fairly bleak period in the town's fortunes compared with previous decades and its shops and inns came to depend more and more on local trade for survival. Fortunately this trade was very much on the increase and the population actually grew between 1861 and 1871 as the railway brought new residents to the town. Kelly's Directories of the period described the situation of the town as 'in the valley of the Wey, the surrounding lofty hills, which are beautifully wooded, and the views from which are extensive and picturesque, render the town and neighbourhood attractive places of residences'.

Charterhouse School, which had been founded in London in 1611, moved to Godalming in 1872 and impressive buildings were constructed of Bargate stone with Bath stone dressings to the north of the town. This increased the desirability of Godalming as a residential centre and the next forty years saw the rapid expansion of suburbs. For example, Croft Road, Latimer Road and Town End Street were built to the south, each following, at least in part, the course of an earlier track or footpath. Substantial residences were built on Frith Hill to the north and the small village of Farncombe expanded rapidly. Houses were built in Peperharow Road, originally for the masters of Charterhouse, and in one of these the writer Aldous Huxley was born in 1894, his father being a master at the school.

Other changes took place in the town centre in addition to the construction of South Street to join up with the new Croft Road and the building of Queen Street which entailed the demolition of properties in the High Street. Station Road was cut across land adjacent to the Mill

Charterhouse School about 1900, an impressive Victorian edifice built mainly of local bargate stone and opened in 1872.

Lane Tannery to join Harts Lane which was later renamed Mint Street. Several significant new buildings were erected including the large Congregational Church in Bridge Street in 1868 and the now demolished Masonic Hall in South Street in 1886. This building is of interest as it was constructed of mainly brick, a break from the traditional use of Bargate stone. Bargate stone was becoming unfashionable and local quarrying for building stone declined as a result.

The rapid increase in population led to the rise of a new type of Godalming 'entrepreneur', of whom Charles Burgess, who took over a grocery business in the High Street about 1873, is a good example. His business soon prospered and by 1885 he had two branches, also in the High Street. Further success followed and by the 1900s there were Burgess's Stores in Haslemere, Milford, Farncombe, Hindhead, Liphook, Guildford and Shottermill in additon to those in Godalming. As a leading trader in the town, Burgess naturally involved himself in local politics. He served the town for fifty years and was six times elected Mayor, firstly in 1884 and lastly in 1926. Burgess's Stores continued to offer unrivalled service until the 1960s. In 1885 their catalogue offered everything from biscuits to pipe clay.

Thomas Rea was another who gave loyal service to the town being

The aproned figure standing in the doorway of 29 High Street may be E.W Chilman who ran a grocer's business here until 1884. No.30 on the extreme left of the photograph, was the premises of John Hull Brown, tea dealer, ale, wine, and beer merchant. Chilman's son moved next door in 1889 and vacated No.29 which by 1901 had become E.D. Brown's Godalming Nurseries. After 1889 Chilman traded only as a wine and spirit merchant and beer bottler, opening a branch in Haslemere. No.28 to the right, was occupied by G. Holden, boot and shoe manufacturer. The High Street was renumbered in about 1964 and the two shops in this fascinating 17th century building became numbers 74 and 76.

elected Mayor on several occasions. Rea owned the 'Oak Bark Tannery' in Mill Lane and also had a butcher's shop in the High Street. He was a J.P. and a leading member of the Congregational Church for fifty years. E.W. Chilman started in business as a grocer but later became more well known as a wine and spirit merchant and beer bottler. Supplying the increasing population with drink proved to be very lucrative and the firm of Chilman's soon opened a second branch in Haslemere.

Many others like Chilman benefited financially by attending to the thirst of the inhabitants. In 1885 there were no less than twenty-three inns and beerhouses, three hotels, six wine and spirit merchants and two beer sellers recorded in the local directory. This list does not include a further six inns and beerhouses and one hotel in Meadrow. The four breweries in Bridge Street have been mentioned earlier in this chapter but there were also two mineral water manufacturers operating at this time. Drunkenness was something of a problem and it was reported in 1892 in a return to the licencing magistrates that the landlords of both 'The

Cornmeter' in Church Street and 'The Red Lion' had recently been convicted of allowing drunkenness on their premises. In contrast 'The Rose and Crown' was 'excellently directed' and 'The Star Inn' 'very well watched over' by their respective landlords. With these ample opportunities to obtain alcoholic refreshment it is not surprising that in contrast there was also a strong temperance movement in the town. For the benefit of the teetotaller John Jasper Taylor who ran 'The Angel' in the High Street was also proprietor of a temperance hotel in Deanery House in Church Street.

Improved living conditions brought about by a new-found knowledge of the value of basic hygiene meant that the death rate fell considerably by 1900. This was especially true of children where the number in earlier generations who died in infancy was tragically high. John Woods, who died in the smallpox epidemic of 1739, was a clothier who had eight

A Christmas display outside Charles Burgess's Borough Stores in the 1900s. The shop on the extreme right was demolished only a few years ago to allow for the widening of Moss Lane. The facade of the rest of the building has been retained as part of the modern shop of Boots the Chemist.

F. & A. Berry, grocers, were in business at 107, High Street between 1887 and 1891. Next door to them was the shop of G. Johnson, chemist and mineral water manufacturer. The third building on the left was demolished in 1897 to make way for Queen Street.

children. Four of them died before the age of five, one was still-born and only one reached maturity and married. The children of the town may have received some form of education even prior to 1670 at the 'Towne School' and there was a Parochial Charity School in existence by 1724. In 1813 the 'Bell School' opened in a two-storey building at The Mint off Mill Lane. Education at the school was based on the methods of Dr Andrew Bell. A 'British School' using the rival methods of Joseph Lancaster was established in Bridge Road. The Bell School moved to the old parish workhouse in Moss Lane in 1843 and a County First School still occupies the site. The original Godalming Grammar School is now the public bar of 'The Red Lion'.

In 1881 Godalming made its mark when the Corporation decided that its borough should be illuminated by electric light. The electricity came from a generator driven by a 13½ foot water-wheel at the leather mill at Westbrook. Lighting had previously been by gas and a gas company had been founded in the town in 1836. The generator at Westbrook Mill constituted the first public power station and the birth of the electricity supply industy. It was not a great success, however, and the street lighting reverted to gas in 1884 but the stage had been set and, once the system had

On November 12th 1881 *The Graphic* announced to the world the new wonder of electric street lighting.

been perfected, it soon ousted gas lighting in streets throughout the world.

The end of the nineteenth century saw the rapid rise in the popularity of the bicycle which gave the individual a previously unknown freedom of travel. Godalming, surrounded by beautiful countryside, became a popular centre for touring and many of the town's inns and hotels catered especially for the cyclist. This new found freedom of the open road was not to last long, for the first motorcars were soon to make their appearance in Godalming. The coming of the automobile in many ways epitomized the coming of a new age and the end of a relaxed, slower way of life which to the modern romantic seems infinitely more appealing.

Famous and Infamous Godhelmians

Every town in England has through the centuries been the home or birthplace of men and women who have found fame outside its confines. In the history of Godalming there have been many such people, characters of national importance, characters of infamy, but all with lives of fascination in the retelling. Indeed, Godalming has so many that any short chapter of their biographies must needs be selective.

Probably one of the most well known Godalming residents was General James Oglethorpe, founder of the State of Georgia in the U.S.A. The Oglethorpe connection with Godalming began when James's father, Sir Theophilus Oglethorpe, bought the Westbrook estate in 1688. James was born in London on 22nd December 1696, the youngest of Sir Theophilus's three surviving sons. The oldest son, Lewis, died as a result of a battle wound at The Hague in 1704 and the other son, Theophilus junior, relinquished all his titles to follow the Jacobite cause abroad. Theophilus senior had died in 1702 and in 1718 James Edward became squire of Westbrook. He was elected as one of the two M.P.s for Haslemere in 1722 and in Parliament James soon acquired a reputation as a social reformer, particularly in respect of prisons. His interest was first aroused when a friend died of smallpox in a debtors' prison. In 1729 he was appointed chairman of a committee to investigate the prison problem and a catalogue of bribery and cruelty was revealed in their reports. This work sowed the seeds of the idea that colonisation could be a remedy for the worst ills of poverty. Despite all his Parliamentary work, James took a keen interest in the local affairs of Godalming and is said to have been very popular locally. In 1729, for example, he contributed a guinea towards repairs to the Market House.

In 1732 James's dream of establishing a colony in America became reality when he sailed with 120 settlers to a tract of land between the Rivers Savannah and Alatamaha. Many of the settlers were ex-prisoners but most of the problems this may have caused seem to have been overcome by James's natural qualities of leadership. The new colony was called Georgia, after King George II, and the town of Savannah was soon established. Further settlers arrived including a number of German speaking protestants who had been banished from the Salzburg area of Austria.

In 1734 James returned to England and brought with him ten Indians of

Westbrook House in 1853, formerly the home of James Oglethorpe. This view shows the house much as it must have looked following additions made by Nathaniel Godbold, inventor of the famous vegetable balsam, who bought the house in 1790.

the Yamacraw tribe including their chief, Tomochichi. In Godalming the appearance of the Indians caused quite a stir and people came from miles around to see them at the 'White Hart'. Unfortunately this was the time of the great smallpox epidemics in the town and when one of the Indians caught the dread disease and died, the others isolated themselves in Westbrook.

In October 1735, James sailed again for Georgia taking with him the Wesley brothers, John and Charles. The possibility of war with Spain seriously threatened the future of the colony as the Spaniards were established in Florida to the south. However James's skills as a soldier, learnt as a young man whilst serving under Prince Eugene in Germany and Hungary, resulted in a successful campaign against larger forces which ensured the safety of his infant colony. Much of the cost had been met from his own funds and the Lords of the Treasury refused to reimburse all of the expenditure, with the result that James was forced to mortgage Westbrook to stave off bankruptcy.

In February 1743 he was promoted to the rank of brigadier-general and later in the same year returned to England. He married an heiress, Elizabeth Wright, a marriage which went a long way to solving his financial problems. James had returned to raise more troops to defend

Georgia but the Jacobite Rising of 1745 intervened to upset his plans and he and his soldiers were diverted to join the Duke of Cumberland, whose forces were harassing the retreating Jacobites. James and the Duke were totally incompatible characters and, such was the Duke's dislike for his fellow soldier no doubt born of jealousy for the other's obviously superior talent, that he lodged a charge of misconduct. An apocryphal story which was current at the time was that James was caught on the eve of Culloden in possession of 'treasonable correspondence' and fled to Westbrook which he proceeded to fortify. In fact fortifications like 'Little Fort', which still stands as a private house on the hillside above Westbrook, were built while James was still in America at the instigation of James' sister, Anne, a known Jacobite sympathiser. Cumberland's charge was that the General had 'lingered on the road' and thereby failed fully to follow up and destroy the retreating Jacobites. There may be some grain of truth in the charge as James would naturally have abhorred the type of unnecessary butchery which the Duke of Cumberland delighted in.

Although acquitted at the court-martial, James' soldiering was at an end. He did not return to Georgia but once again took an active role in Parliament, as throughout all his other adventures he had still remained M.P. for Haslemere. His parliamentary career ended abruptly in 1754 when he was defeated at the election and he retired from public life to his wife's home at Cranham Hall in Essex. He seems rarely if ever to have returned to Westbrook and for much of the next thirty years the house was shuttered and closed. He died at Cranham in 1785 in his eighty-ninth year, immortalized in Pope's famous couplet: 'One, driven by strong benevolence of soul, Shall fly like Oglethorpe from pole to pole.'

If James Oglethorpe was the 'famous man' of eighteenth century Godalming, then Mary Toft was the 'infamous woman' at the centre of a scandal which excited the interest of the whole nation in 1726. Mary, who worked in a hop-garden near the Ockford Road, was described as a simple minded woman, wife of a poor journeyman clothier, Joshua Toft. She was pregnant through the summer and autumn of 1726 and at the birth in November she was attended by the local midwife and a Doctor Howard of Guildford. After the birth, Doctor Howard amazed the local population by claiming that he had delivered Mary of eighteen rabbits! Apparently she had been 'frightened' by rabbits in the fields the previous April and this was the explanation for this extraordinary birth. The news of the birth soon spread throughout England and reached the ears of King George I who ordered the royal physicians to investigate the matter. There was much serious argument though many, including Hogarth who drew a caricature of the birth, realised what a ridiculous fraud it all was. The whole incident was eventually exposed and Mary Toft was committed to the county gaol, still protesting her innocence. She spent only a short time in prison for by 4th February 1728 she had returned to her home where she gave birth to an 'ordinary' child. 'Being the first child after her pretending rabbett breeding' wrote the vicar in the parish register beside the record of the child's baptism.

Gertrude Jekyll, who lived at Munstead, was a well-known figure in the town during the late nineteenth and early twentieth century. Much has already been written about her unique talent as a garden designer and her years of collaboration with Edwin Lutyens, the famous architect who was born at Thursley. In her earlier years before her eyes deteriorated she was very much involved in furnishings, embroidery and interior decoration. She was also a writer and had a number of books on gardening published. In addition she wrote two fascinating books on country and cottage life in which she faithfully recorded details of a vanishing heritage in a way which was many years ahead of its time. The chapter on Godalming in 'Old West Surrey' which was published in 1904, contains the following call for planning laws and conservation areas: 'Even from the point of view of commercial convenience and well-being it would be well if there could be some strict censorship exercised in the matter of the removal or rebuilding of houses in such conspicuous positions as the streets of country towns.' In recent times one town adjacent to Godalming could well have paid heed to Gertrude Jekyll. Gertrude Jekyll is also

Jack Phillips, hero of the RMS Titanic's tragic final hours in April 1912.

Hogarth's contemporary cartoon satirising the Mary Toft rabbit breeding scandal in 1726.

remembered in Godalming as the designer of the gardens of the Phillips Memorial Cloister, which was built on land between the church and river to plans by Hugh Thackeray Turner in memory of John George Phillips.

When the Titanic hit an iceberg in the Atlantic whilst on her maiden voyage in April 1912 on board, as chief wireless operator, was 'Jack' Phillips, a local man who had been born in Farncombe. His father and mother managed a branch of Gammons, the Godalming drapers, in Farncombe Street and Jack had attended Godalming Grammar School and also sung in Farncombe Church choir as a boy. The story of Jack Phillips's last hours became a national legend. Phillips stayed at his post, sending the distress signal to the last and thus sacrificed his life. We still live in a time when the best remembered hero is a dead one and this was certainly true of Jack Phillips. In fact there was a second wireless operator assisting Phillips in the transmission of the SOS and both left the 'Marconi Room' at the same time on the instructions of the captain. This second operator, Harold Bride, survived and had this to say at the official American inquiry: 'Leaving the cabin, we climbed on top of the houses comprising the officers' quarters and our own, and here I saw the last of

Mr Phillips, for he disappeared walking aft'. Bride is now a forgotten hero of that tragic night in April 1912, an acceptable price for having survived.

Godalming was also the birthplace of another hero of the seas, Admiral Sir John Balchin. Balchin was born in the town on 4th February 1670 and joined the navy at the age of fourteen. He gradually advanced through the ranks and eventually commanded a number of ships during a long career spanning sixty years. In 1744 he was knighted and retired with a pension. At the age of seventy-five most people would have quietly accepted this honourable retirement but not Balchin. In July of the same year he sailed in the Victory (not Nelson's) in command of a squadron ordered to relieve a force which was blockaded in the mouth of the River Tagus by the French. The mission was entirely successful but during the return journey a violent storm blew up, the squadron was scattered and 'Victory' with, it is said, over a thousand people on board, was never seen again. Thus was lost a real naval hero in every sense of the word.

At the opposite end of the scale of human qualities mention must be made of the infamous murderers Chennell and Chalcraft, who in 1817 committed a particularly grisly murder in the town. After getting drunk one night, they returned to Chennell's father's home and bludgeoned the poor man and his housekeeper to death. No motive for this horrible crime was put forward other than that of petty theft. The two criminals were soon apprehended and sent for trial at the Guildford Assizes in August 1818 where, according to several reports, almost the entire population of Godalming flocked for the trial. Chennell and Chalcraft were found guilty and brought back to Godalming to be hanged. Several thousand people came to witness Godalming's last public execution on the Lammas Lands to the north of the town. Some say that the horseshoe shaped depression in the meadows, which is still visible today, is the spot where this vast crowd stood. In reality it is probably the remains of a silted-up channel of the river.

Godalming has produced several sportsmen of renown and in the nineteenth century was most famed for its cricketers, several members of the Caesar family being the most well known. Of the Caesars it was Julius who had a successful career as a professional cricketer but a career brought to an end by tragedy. Julius was born in 1830, the seventh child of a Godalming baker, Benjamin Caesar and his wife Ann. Incidentally, his mother's maiden name had been Bowler! The Caesars were a large family with a great tradition of cricket; in 1850 twelve of the family played a team of eleven 'gentlemen' of Godalming but were surprisingly beaten.

Julius's own special talent as a batsman was soon recognised and in 1849 he joined Surrey County Cricket Club. In 1859 he was selected for the first England eleven to tour abroad and the party, which went to Canada and U.S.A., remained unbeaten even when playing against

Vice Admiral Sir John Balchin was born of very obscure Parentage February 4th 1669 at Godalming in Surrey, and rose to the Eminence noticed above solely by his own Exertions and Services, for which he was rewarded by his Sovereign with the Governorship of Greenwich Hospital. This distinguished Officer was unhappily lost in October 1744 off Alderney with the whole of the Crew 1200 in Number having his Flag then on board the Victory of 110 Guns. A Monument still exists in Westminster Abbey to his Memory.

John Balchin, a famous son of the town whose distinguished career in the navy led him from humble beginnings to national fame. The date of his birth on this illustration is based on the old style calendar.

teams of twenty-two. During the winter of 1863-64 Julius was in the team which also remained unbeaten throughout the tour of Australia. Unfortunately tragedy struck when a gun he was carrying on a pheasant shoot near Godalming went off, accidently killing one of the beaters. Julius was so profoundly shocked by this incident that it affected his game which deteriorated rapidly. He retired in 1867 to concentrate on his business as a cricketers' outfitter which he ran from his home in Ockford Road (the house is now demolished).

In 1872 Charterhouse moved to Godalming and Julius was appointed coach and supplier of cricket equipment to the school. This good fortune was not to last long as futher tragedy was soon to strike. His wife died in 1874 and in 1876 his second son, Julius, committed suicide by throwing himself in front of a train on the line north of Godalming. Poor Julius never recovered from these two further blows and took to the bottle. He died on 5th March 1878 in the 'Railway Tavern', adjacent to the 'new' station, where he was lodging. The building still stands but is now 'Arden House'. Julius was buried in the Nightingale Road cemetery but no stone marks his grave, a sad end for a famous cricketer who played with all the greats of his time including a youthful W.G. Grace.

The Moss Lane fire engine house built in 1816, vacated by the brigade in the 1870s and demolished about 60 years ago.

The Twentieth Century and the Town Today

The expansion of Godalming which began in the mid-nineteenth century has continued apace throughout much of the last eighty years. Between 1901 and 1981 the population more than doubled, largely because of the town's popularity as a residential area. Craddock's Godalming Almanac and Directory of 1900 gave a foretaste of this growth when it said of the town: 'During the last few years building operations have been carried on very extensively in the town and neighbourhood. The demand for residences, is daily increasing – the general salubrity of the locality, and the facility of railway accommodation, offering great inducements for families desiring convenient country residences'. These new homes were built mainly to the north and south of the old town centre, outside the boundaries of the original borough which were then extended successively to encompass them. Farncombe was brought into the borough in 1892 while further areas were added in 1928 and 1933.

The increase in population was also reflected in the construction of several new public buildings in the 1900s including the Roman Catholic Church in Croft Road, the municipal buildings in Bridge Street and the Fire Station in Queen Street. The original engine house for the voluntary fire brigade was in Moss Lane but in the late 1870s a new house was built in Wharf Street. In 1904 the brigade moved to Queen Street where they remained for many years until the present modern fire station was constructed in Bridge Road.

The town was certainly in need of an efficient fire service as it suffered a series of disastrous fires, the first being soon after the brigade moved to Queen Street. In the early hours of Tuesday, 7th March 1905 fire broke out at the Oak Bark Tannery in Mill Lane. During the preceding two decades the tannery had been greatly expanded and now covered several acres including premises on both sides of the lane which were connected by a galvanised iron and concrete bridge. The Godalming Fire Brigade was quickly summoned by the usual sounding of the hooter at the gasworks, which could be heard throughout the town. With the help of the Guildford Brigade which arrived later to give assistance, they managed to confine the fire to a large five-storey building adjacent to the River Ock. This building was completely destroyed, parts of it collapsing onto a nearby cottage or falling into the lane. At its height the fire illuminated the whole town and could be seen for miles around.

There was a considerable amount of building on the outskirts of the town at the turn of the century as these views illustrate. Pepperharow Road and Dean Road as seen from Frith Hill in about 1900 have a scatter of new houses and also building plots in preparation, whilst the houses seen at the end of Borough Road had only recently been built.

Fortunately the damaged cottage was repaired and still stands today, as does Hatch Mill which was badly scorched by the flames. Less fortunately the fire was a blow to one of the town's major industries and many men were thrown out of work.

The leather trade, which had been carried on in the town at least since the fifteenth century received another setback when Pullman's Leather Mills at Westbrook caught fire on 9th December 1914 and was severely damaged. Leather and skin working continued at Westbrook on an ever decreasing scale until after the Second World War but its heyday was gone forever.

By the time of the Westbrook fire most of the inhabitants' attention was becoming focused on the disastrous holocaust of the First World War. Hundreds of acres to the south of the town were turned into huge army camps like that at Witley Common. The influx of thousands of troops into the area must have been viewed with mixed feelings by the townspeople,

Godalming Fire Brigade outside the fire station in Queen Street. The station was built by David Fry, the firm being based in an ex-brewery yard in Bridge Street, and was opened on 4th May 1904. This photograph may well have been taken about that time. The brigade would certainly have been keen to show off their new steamer, the purchase of which coincided with the move from the old and unsuitable rented engine house in Wharf Street.

Fire at Messrs Pullman's. Dec. 9th 1914.

A spectacular picture of the disastrous fire at Westbrook Mill. On the right bank of the river stands the town fire brigade's steamer with a large pipe reaching down to bring water from the stream. In circumstances such as this huge conflagration the brigade was powerless to do anything but contain the fire to those portions of the premises already ablaze.

but they soon rallied round to assist in any way possible. Sometimes trains would disgorge hundreds of soldiers at Godalming Station where, before marching to camp, they would be refreshed by cups of tea brewed by local helpers. Witley Camp became a depot for Canadian troops who were regularly in the town; a canteen for them was established in Croft Road. The soldiers played games of various sorts with the townspeople, especially the girls, several of whom eventually married Canadians. Some local inhabitants still remember the Canadians skating and playing ice-hockey on Broadwater Lake. Contact with the troops was not always a pleasant experience and military police regularly patrolled the town to arrest trouble-makers.

Many of the tradesmen must have benefited from the influx of thousands of extra customers and some even established branches along the Portsmouth Road near Witley Camp. These temporary shops were built of galavanised iron and wood and the area became known as 'Tin Town'. One enterprising tradesman even established the 'Ottawa Cafe' in the High Street. After the war, local 'profiteering committees' were set up throughout the country to investigate allegations of unreasonable profits accumulated from the war, no doubt the symptom of a nation's guilty conscience for the hundreds of thousands who had died. Few escaped the committee's attention in Godalming and even the redoubtable Alderman Charles Burgess was found to have charged one lady a penny too much for her ginger!

Towards the end of the war, the town was hit by the great Spanish flu epidemic, otherwise known as 'the plague of the Spanish lady', which swept through Europe and eventually carried off more people than were killed in the fighting. Godalming fared no better than most and a number of its inhabitants died. The local schools were closed for long periods when the epidemic was at its worst during the autumn of 1918 and into 1919.

After the Armistice in November 1918 the giant 'war machine' took a long time to run down and Canadian troops in the local camps became more and more frustrated at the delays in being sent home. This frustration finally boiled over in June 1919 when the local troops at Witley Camp rioted and totally wrecked 'Tin Town'. Godalming was more fortunate than Epsom where, during the same week, Canadian soldiers seriously damaged the town's police station and killed a police sergeant. Eventually Witley Camp was disbanded and Godalming tried to return to normal but a whole way of life seemed to have gone beyond recall. The town's dead were commemorated by a memorial near the Phillips' Cloister close to the church and in 1925 a chapel was built at Charterhouse in memory of the many old boys of the School who were killed.

During the 1920s mass production brought the motor car within the reach of an ever increasing number of the population and the narrow streets of Godalming began to become choked with traffic, a problem which has stayed with the town ever since. Even before and during the war the Surrey Advertiser regularly carried reports of the tragic death of some unsuspecting pedestrian, especially children, who, being used to walking leisurely in the road, had been mown down by a new chariot of the highway. In 1932 the Guildford and Godalming By-pass was constructed to the west of the town but it proved to be only partial solution to the choking traffic. After much planning and discussion during the last forty years, a new road to relieve the High Street of traffic was eventually built to the south of the High Street with a spur running from Station Road across the Mint Street carpark, to the Ockford Road. Called Flambard Way, after that arch-rogue Rannulf Flambard, many would, no doubt, consider the road aptly named.

The period between the wars saw further house building on the outskirts of the town, especially those constructed by the Corporation on estates such as Ockford Ridge. Such building highlighted a trend which had really started in the nineteenth century, a population movement away from the old town centre to new clean and healthy suburbs mainly situated in the surrounding hills. Many of the 'backyard' areas of old Godalming gradually became rundown and were finally demolished. Cottages have disappeared from Mint Street, The Mint, Wharf Street and Ockford Road, for example. Several more significant properties have also been lost including those at the top of Bridge Street opposite the 'Sun' and the building in the High Street which was occupied by Jones the Ironmongers for many years. This shop, with its prominent carriage entrance giving access to the rear, had been an ironmongers for well over a hundred years, having been previously run by the Norris family. Its

Bridge Street in about 1860 showing the house variously known as Coles, Frenches, or King John's Hunting Lodge, although it is most unlikely to have ever had any connection with that unfortunate king. The house was burnt down in 1869. The large plane tree seen in the distance was a prominent feature of this end of the town until it was cut down in February 1968.

characterless replacement is certainly no worthy substitute. Many properties have also been lost in the area of Bridge Street near the town bridge including Bridge House which was for many years occupied by members of the Marshall family. A large plane tree which was a prominent feature of this end of the town was cut down in the late 1960s and this whole area is now a sad skeleton of its former self.

It seemed that, no sooner had the country as a whole recovered from the 1914-18 War and the Depression of the Thirties, than another World War was upon it. In the Godalming area the old army camps such as Witley Common thrived once again. The 1939-45 War brought a new terror to the civilian population in the form of mass bombing raids. Some hint of the horrors to come had been apparent in the First World War when Zeppelin airships had been responsible for the first civilian air-raid casualties in the country. Godalming took precautions in 1916 with the setting up of a committee which made various plans in case of a raid which fortunately proved unnecessary. However, in the Second World War the town was not so fortunate and a total of 213 bombs of various types fell on or near built-up areas. Five buildings were totally destroyed including two cottages in Catteshall Lane and another thirty-nine severely damaged. In 1941 four bombs fell on Charterhouse but the School had a lucky escape and damage was relatively minor. Later in the war two flying bombs dropped on the borough, one on The Wharf and the other on Holloway Hill. Miraculously no civilians were killed in any of these raids but an army officer and an N.C.O. died when an unexploded bomb they were removing from a garden in Hurtmore Road suddenly detonated.

V-E Day in 1945 brought great celebrations with much bunting and flags and many parties. Godalming was already famous for the lavish scale of its public celebrations, starting with those for Queen Victoria's Jubilees in 1887 and 1897 when imposing archways were constructed across the High Street. When the Duchess of Albany came to open the Meath Home in 1892, the entire town was covered in flags and banners. The Home for epileptic women was founded by the Countess of Meath at Westbrook, which had previously been the home of James Oglethorpe and then Nathaniel Godbold, inventor of the famous vegetable balsam. Preparations for the Coronation of King George the Sixth in 1937 were on a vast scale. Arches were built over the Town Bridge and a huge procession organised to march from the Ockford Road through the town to Farncombe and then to Broadwater, where there would be many other entertainments. In the event, a huge downpour wrecked the parade, which was finally postponed until the following Monday, the Whit Bank Holiday. This tradition of town parades is now continued every year at the time of the town fete and in 1981 the parade was for a very special centenary—that of the world's first public electricity supply service at

Celebrations in Church Street for the opening of the Meath Home by the Duchess of Albany on 4th August 1892. The building on the left, behind the woman in the white apron, was the Cornmeter pub. Just visible on its side wall is a sign referring to the Wesleyan Chapel in Harts Lane, now Mint Street, occupied today by the Salvation Army.

Godalming in 1881. Since the last war, Godalming has continued to prosper with much building, especially on Frith Hill and most recently near Shackstead Lane. A number of the large nineteenth century residences have been demolished in favour of smaller dwellings or flats. To a great extent the small shopkeeper has given way to supermarkets and branches of national companies, and factories have been replaced by offices. The offices in Ockford Road, originally built as Panda House, are a pleasing example of well designed modern architecture. Not all the town's recent buildings can be described in this way but it is essential that some of the old must give way to the new if the town is not to become a 'fossil'. Godalming is indeed fortunate that it has not suffered the wholesale redevelopment inflicted upon some Surrey towns and the basic character has been very much retained.

In April 1974 Godalming became part of the new Waverley District, comprising most of South-west Surrey including Farnham and Haslemere. Thus it lost its borough status just a few months short of its 400th anniversary. The traditions of the borough are still continued, however, by a very active town council whose leader still holds the title of Mayor. Waverley Borough Council has also made the town its headquarters with the construction of offices in Bridge Street.

In September 1977 Waverley District twinned with the Mayen-Koblenz District of Germany and this friendship was further cemented when, in April 1982, a 'Deed of Partnership' was signed by the Town Mayor of Godalming and the Oberburgermeister of Mayen. The town is now also twinned with Joigny in France. Numerous exchange visits have been organised between the towns, Godalming being no stranger to overseas visitors, as it has regularly received parties from Georgia over the years. These many visitors have soon come to appreciate Godalming's character and the pride most of its people have for the place in which they live.

Change has come to Godalming during the last decade in a way not seen since the coming of the railway a century and a half ago. The building of the Relief Road has removed the choking traffic from its ancient centre and an enhancement scheme will once again make the town a pleasant place in which to stroll and shop. The early 1990s has been a period of economic decline but this is nothing new. The town has survived recession many times during its long history and will do so again.

The majority of Godhelmians have always cared greatly about their town and have come to love its individuality, the uniqueness of its narrow winding streets and its thriving sense of community. I hope that in some way this story of Godalming, although merely a brief glimpse of a fascinating history, will help many more to appreciate this ancient town.

Further Reading

This list contains details of works which are still generally available. Much further material of great interest is housed in Godalming Museum including the Woods' Manuscript Collection which was bequeathed to the town when Percy Woods died in 1922.

BOTT, Alan – A Guide to the Parish Church of Saint Peter and Saint Paul, Godalming.
Parochial Church Council, 1987.

COOMBS, David (editor) – Godalming 400: moments in history.
Godalming 400 Committee, 1974.

COOMBS, David (editor) – Memories of Farncombe and Godalming.
The Godalming Trust, 1981.

CROCKER, Alan & Glenys – Catteshall Mill: a survey of the history and archaeology of an industrial site at Godalming, Surrey.
Surrey Archaeological Society, 1981.

HAVERON, Francis – The Brilliant Ray or How the Electric Light was Brought to Godalming in 1881.
Godalming Electricity Centenary Celebrations Committee, 1981.

HEAD, R.E.—Godalming in Old Picture Postcards. European Library, 1984.

HEAD, R.E.—Godalming in Old Picture Postcards Volume 2. European Library, 1990.

JANAWAY, John—Godalming (Yesterday's Town Series). Barracuda Books, 1987.

Victoria History of the County of Surrey Volume 3
Constable, 1911.

Index

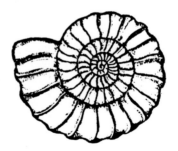

For full details of our publications please write to:

Ammonite Books
58 Coopers Rise
Godalming
Surrey GU7 2NJ